Alien Adventures

WOOD STREET COUNTY
INFANT SCHOOL
GUILDFORD

The Ruby Cage

Karen Ball ● Jonatronix

OXFORD
UNIVERSITY PRESS

Max's mission log

We are travelling through space on board the micro-ship Excelsa with our new friends, Nok and Seven.

We're on a mission to save Planet Exis (Nok's home planet), which is running out of power. We need to collect four fragments that have been hidden throughout the Beta-Prime Galaxy. Together the fragments form the Core of Exis. Only the Core will restore power to the planet.

It's not easy. A space villain called Badlaw wants the power of the Core for himself. His army of robotic Krools is never far behind us!

Fragments collected so far: 1

In our last adventure ...

We landed on Planet Celeston but the ship was damaged. Ant, Tiger and Seven stayed to fix the ship while I went with Cat and Nok to look for the fragment.

We got caught in a mineral storm but managed to find shelter in a cave.

We found a map on the cave wall showing us where the fragment is hidden. As we left, we heard a growling noise from inside the cave.

Chapter 1 – Pyrite panthers

Max, Cat and Nok stood trembling at the mouth of the cave. The growling noise turned into a snarl. Then something leapt towards them.

"Run!" Max shouted. He sped out into the open. Cat and Nok followed close behind.

They hid behind some rocks and watched as two creatures bounded from the cave.

They looked just like big cats, but they had sparkling gold fur. Their eyes were like diamonds and they wore armour studded with rubies.

Nok peered around the rocks. "Pyrite panthers!" he said.

The pyrite panthers lifted their noses to sniff the air.

"They're trying to pick up our scent," Cat whispered.

Suddenly, a huge roar came from deep inside the cave.

"What was that?" cried Cat.

"A Minatroll," Nok said, quietly. "They keep the pyrite panthers as pets."

"I think we should get out of here," Max said, backing away. "Now!"

Pyrite panthers

Information

These big cats have coats covered with gold pyrite crystals. They have diamond-like eyes which makes it difficult for them to see. This means their other senses are much stronger!

Diet

Pyrite panthers are scavengers – they eat what they can find.

Habitat

Pyrite panthers live in caves round the crystal mountains of Celeston.

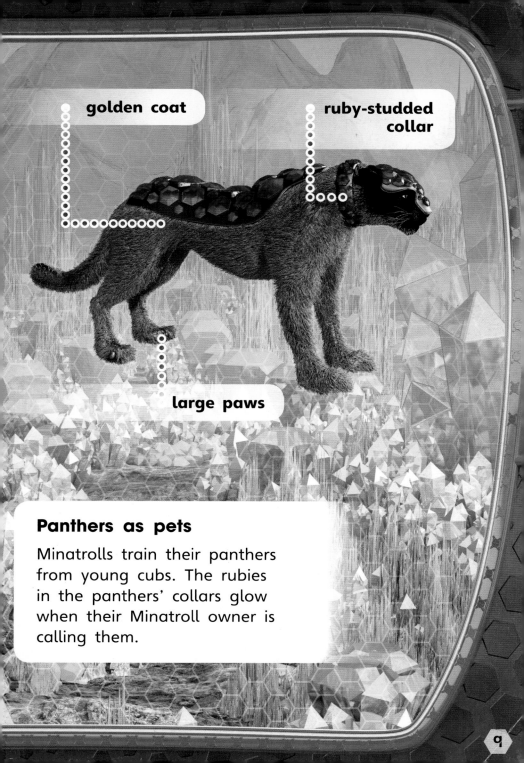

golden coat

ruby-studded collar

large paws

Panthers as pets

Minatrolls train their panthers from young cubs. The rubies in the panthers' collars glow when their Minatroll owner is calling them.

Chapter 2 – Minatroll attack

Max could feel the ground beneath his feet shaking as he ran. He glanced back and saw a huge creature covered in ruby-red armour. It was a Minatroll.

It held its arm up in their direction and shot out a stream of red rays.

"Watch out!" cried Max.

They all ducked as the rays went flying over their heads.

"It's gaining on us," Cat yelled. "We need to go faster."

She pressed the button on her suit to activate her holo-board. Max and Nok followed her lead.

More rays flew towards them. One narrowly missed Max, but it caught the end of Nok's holo-board.

"Help!" cried Nok, as he went crashing to the ground.

Nok rolled over and tried to get to his feet, but he wasn't quick enough. The Minatroll shot out another stream of rays. The rays surrounded Nok and hardened into a ruby cage.

Chapter 3 – No reply

Meanwhile ...

Tiger gazed out of the ship's rear viewscreen at the whirling mineral storm.

"I'm glad we fixed the crack in the power cells before the storm hit," he said. "I hope the others are safe."

"Max," Ant said, pressing the button on
his communi-screen. "Can you hear me?
Can you give me your location?"

All Ant heard was a loud fizzing.
Then there was a screeching noise.
Ant shook his head and switched the
communi-screen off.

Seven looked out at the mineral storm. It was stronger than ever. "The storm must be stopping our communication equipment from working," he said.

"There's nothing we can do but wait until the storm is over then," said Ant.

"I hate waiting!" groaned Tiger.

Chapter 4 – Rescue mission

Max and Cat were hiding behind some large crystals. Cat peered round the edge, but there was no sign of the Minatroll.

"I think we've lost it," she said, breathing hard.

"We have to go back for Nok," Max said. "We can't leave him to face the Minatroll on his own."

"Well," said Cat, pushing off the ground, "what are we waiting for?"

Max grinned and flew up into the air after her.

When they reached Nok, the cage was open. Nok was still inside. He started waving furiously at them.

"Go away!" he shouted.

"We've come to help you," said Cat.

Max and Cat stepped into the cage.

"No, you don't understand," said Nok. "It's a ..."

"TRAP!" roared a voice behind them.

Max and Cat span round to see the Minatroll. It seemed to appear from nowhere.

"It can camouflage itself," said Nok.

The Minatroll laughed as it slammed the cage door shut. They were all trapped inside.

Chapter 5 – Escape

The Minatroll turned round and called
to its panthers.

"Quick," whispered Max. "Shrink down
while it isn't looking."

Max and Cat pressed their buttons and
shrank. They climbed through the bars
and ran.

Cat looked back over her shoulder and saw that Nok wasn't with them. He was still inside the cage. The shrinking button on his suit had failed!

Then the Minatroll let out a huge roar. Another Minatroll appeared at his side.

"Two prisoners have escaped," he said in a gravelly voice. "But we still have one for our collection."

The panthers dragged a huge cart over to the Minatrolls. The cage was loaded on to it.

Max and Cat watched in horror as the pyrite panthers started to tow Nok away. Their mission had just become more difficult than ever.

Find out what happens next in
The Hunt for Nok.